Introducing The Positions...

for VIOLIN—Vol. I THIRD AND FIFTH POSITIONS

There are thousands of students in the public schools of America today, who, after an elementary, class-training in violin playing, restricted entirely to the *first* position of their instrument, have joined the ranks of school orchestras. The purpose of position playing itself, is to extend the tonal range of the violin, and obviously, those students who play only in the first position, by necessity, have no alternative than to remain in elementary ensemble groups, or to play the lower violin parts in intermediate orchestras. They cannot become first violinists in advanced school orchestras because of their inability to play in the higher positions of their instrument. The positions with which these individuals should become acquainted are the *third* and the *fifth*, yet if they turn to traditional violin methods for aid in acquiring a knowledge of the higher positions of which they are in need, they are confronted with an array of ungraded material, starting with the *second* position, and passing directly from the *second* to the *third* position, from the *third* to the *fourth* position, and so on, in numerical order. From a modern pedagogical standpoint, such a procedure is entirely wrong, and obviously, methods written in such a manner are of little or no value to students in the public schools of the present day.

In actuality, *seven* regular positions are employed in playing the violin, in addition to a so-called *half-position*, and an *eighth*, *ninth* and *tenth* position, each of the latter three of which exists only within the scope of very advanced violin technic. In introducing higher positions to students of the violin, the *third* position *at all times* should be given first attention, for not only is it the easiest to play of all the higher positions (due to the convenience afforded one in resting his left hand against the edge of the instrument), but also it is used a great deal more than any of the other higher positions. Furthermore, by going directly from the *first* to the *third* position, the students learn to play positions in the exact manner in which they will use them most frequently in the ordinary run of violin

playing. In addition, from following the procedure of taking up the *third* position before the *second* position, students are given an opportunity to begin at once, the very important study of shifting, which, unfortunately, is neglected in nearly all violin methods dealing with the study of the positions in the traditional manner.

Following the study of the *third* position, the next higher position to be taken up, from a modern, pedagogical standpoint, should be the *fifth* position. After the *third* position, the *fifth* position is not only the easiest to play of all the higher positions (due to its fingering, which is identical with that of the *first* position, only on a string lower), but also after the *third* position, it is actually employed more than any of the other higher positions. Furthermore, by going directly from the *third* to the *fifth* position, the students again learn to play the positions in the exact manner in which they will use them most frequently in the ordinary run of violin playing.

The scope of the present work is purely that of an introduction to the art of position playing, and because it is limited to the needs of violinists in school orchestras, it is not to be assumed that the author advocates neglecting the study of the remaining positions of the violin. It is a fact, that each position of the instrument should be thoroughly studied by all conscientious students of the violin, but notwithstanding this, the *second*, *fourth*, *sixth* and *seventh* positions should *not* be taken up by students until they have acquired an adequate mastery of the *third* and *fifth* positions.

If *Introducing the Positions* proves itself a boon to those ambitious students in quest of material and procedures that will enable them to become better performers on their instrument, and advance to the rank of first violinist in their school orchestras, the writer will feel gratified to know that his humble efforts have been of some educational significance.

Harvey S. Whistler, Ph. D.

RUBANK®

HAL•LEONARD®
CORPORATION
7777 W. BLUEMOUND RD. P.O. BOX 13819 MILWAUKEE, WI 53213

The Third Position

Preparatory Studies in the Key of C Major

⌐——¬ = Half-step; fingers close together

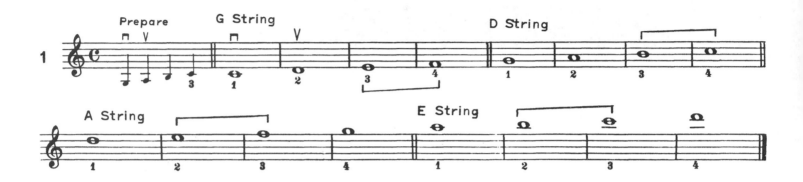

13

Prepare

Test with Open
D String

14

Prepare

Test with Open
D String

15

Prepare

Test with Open
A String

16

Prepare

Test with Open
A String

17

Prepare

Test with Open
A String

Scale Study

18

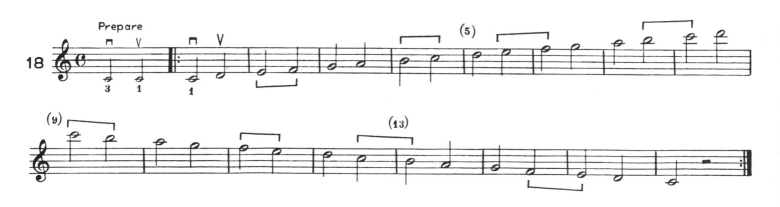

Prepare

Technic Building

Strike fingers forcibly on the strings; listen carefully to intonation.

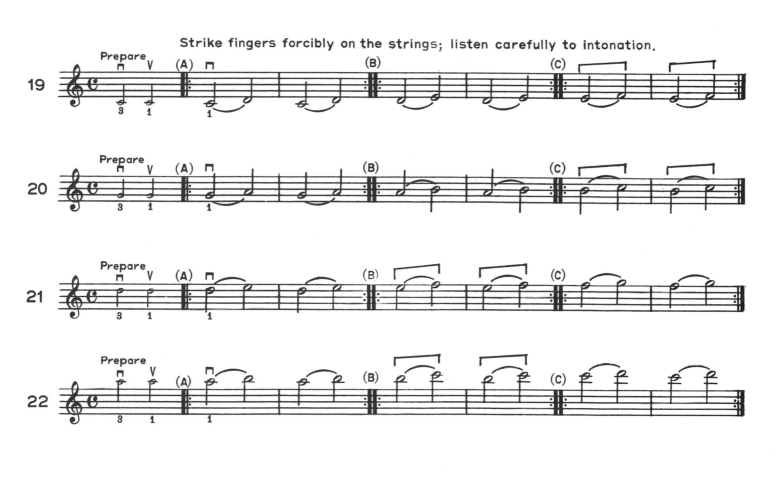

Tone Development

Draw bow slowly; produce a pure, clear tone.

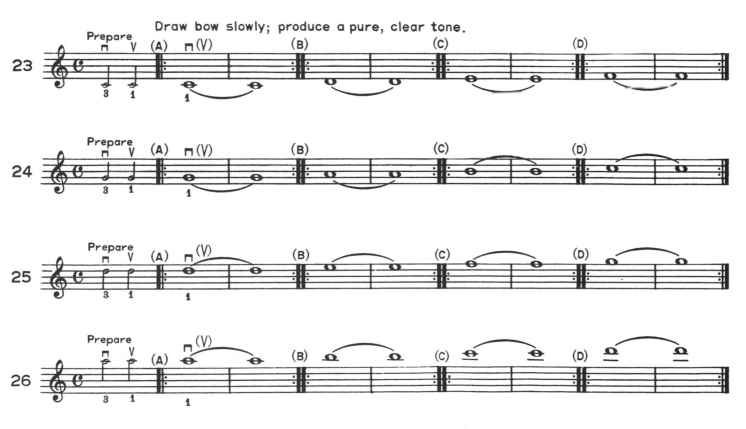

Selected Studies in the Third Position

Shifting from First to Third Position

When shifting from the first to a higher position, do not take the finger up and put it down again; instead, *slide* into the higher position.

G String

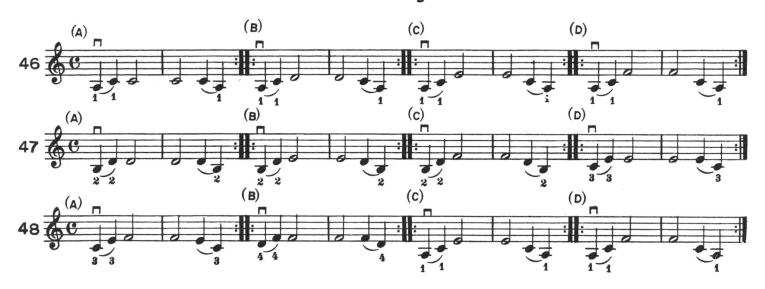

Shifting from One Finger to Another

The student should shift forward on the finger that was last down, and likewise, shift backward on the finger that was last down.

The small note in the following exercises indicates the movement of the finger in shifting, and as the student perfects his ability to shift from one note to another, the small note eventually should not be heard.

Key of G Major

Shifting in Key of G Major

Shifting from One Finger to Another

Key of D Major

Shifting

Advanced Shifting Exercises

SCHOLZ

13

Combining First and Third Positions

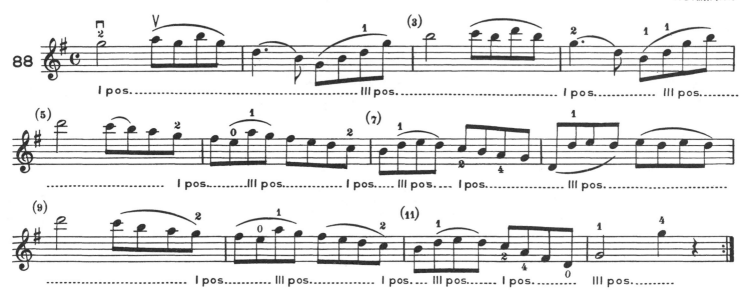

Shifting Studies

SCHOLZ

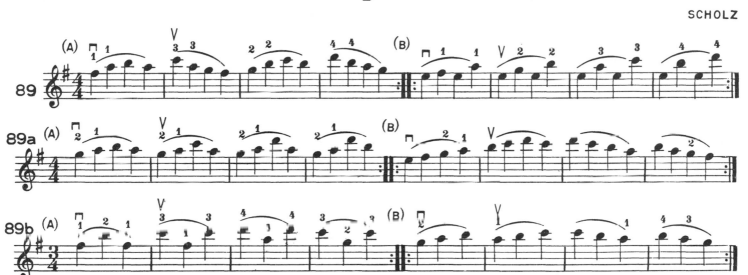

Shifting Studies

DANCLA

Key of F Major

Shifting

Key of B♭ Major

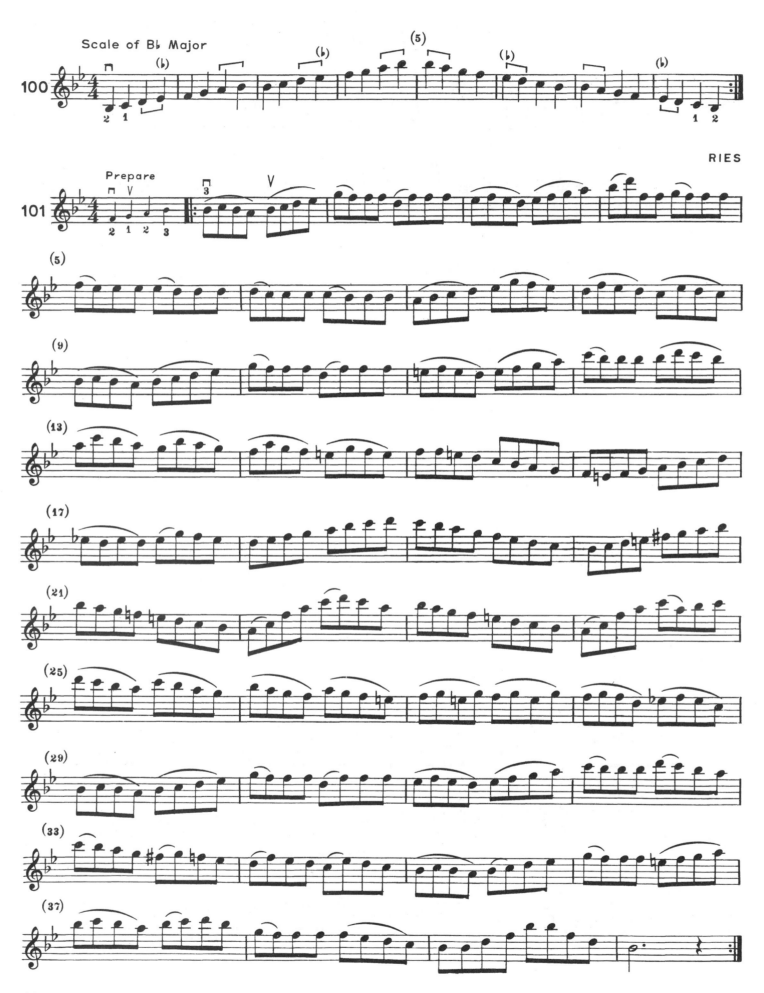

RIES

Shifting

WOHLFAHRT

19

Key of A Major

Shifting

SCHOLZ

WOHLFAHRT

Natural Harmonics

To produce a natural harmonic, merely touch the finger lightly against the string; do not press the finger down. $\frac{4}{0}$ = natural harmonic.

Shifting

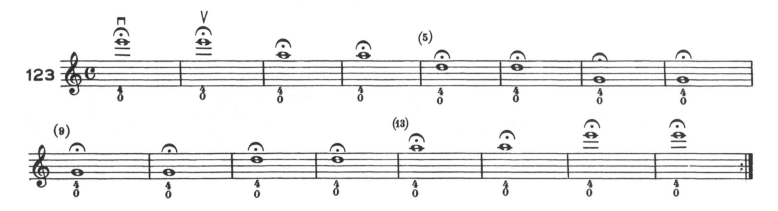

Finger Extensions

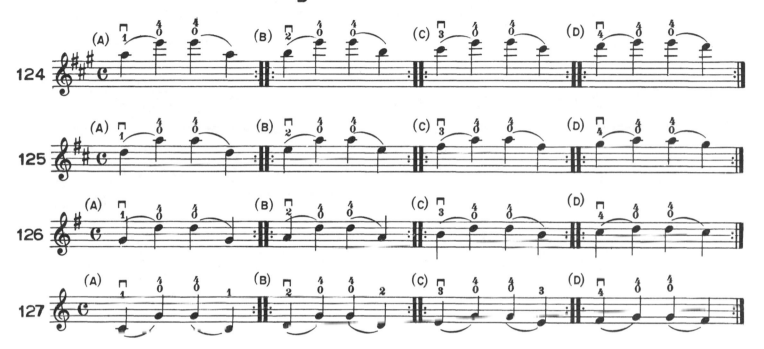

Harmonic Etude

WOHLFAHRT

Key of E♭ Major

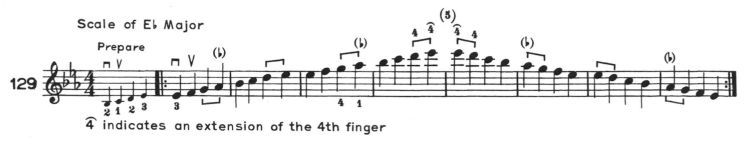

Scale of E♭ Major

129

$\widehat{4}$ indicates an extension of the 4th finger

RIES

130

131

Shifting

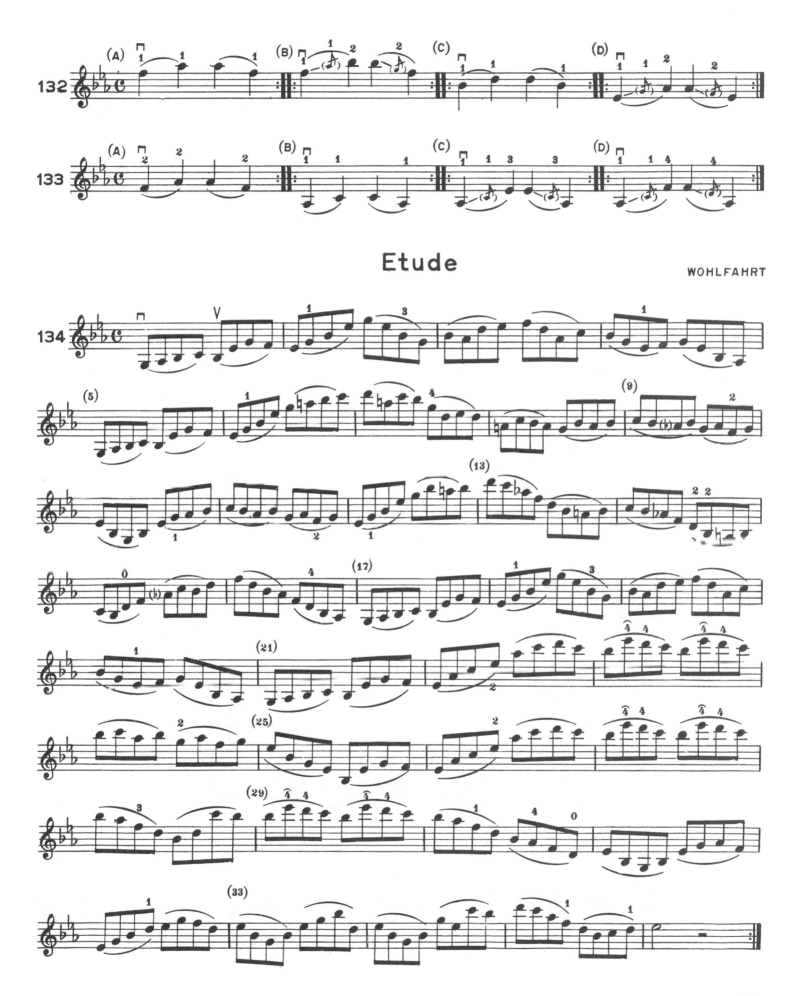

Etude

WOHLFAHRT

Selected Solos in the First and Third Positions

Barcarolle
from Tales of Hoffmann

OFFENBACH

Liebesträume

LISZT

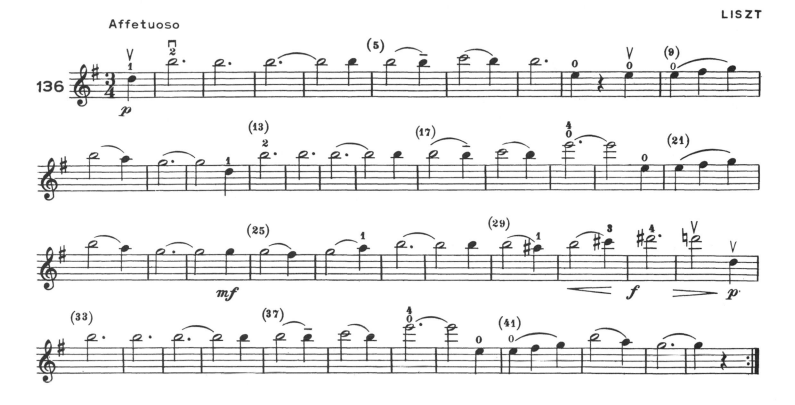

Melody in F

RUBINSTEIN

Merry Widow Waltz

FRANZ LEHAR

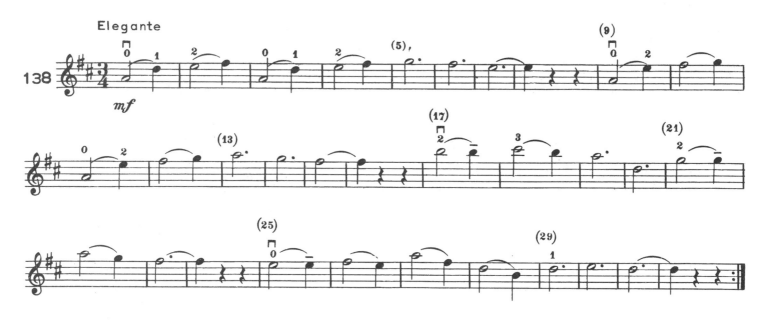

Largo
from New World Symphony

DVORAK

Carry Me Back to Old Virginny

JAMES A. BLAND

Nocturne

Von BLON

The Fifth Position

Preparatory Studies in the Key of C Major

The fingering of the *fifth* position is the same as the fingering of the *first* position (*i.e.*, identical notes require the same fingers), only a string lower, and at a higher place on the fingerboard.

The nearer the strings **are to the bridge of the violin**, the higher they lie above the fingerboard; as a result, when playing in the fifth position, it is essential that the strings are pressed down more forcibly than when playing in lower positions.

De BERIOT

High Tones in the Fifth Position

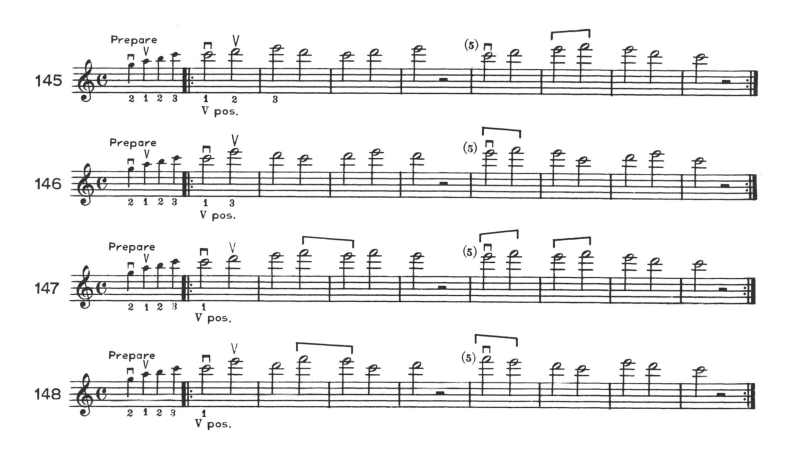

Technic Builder

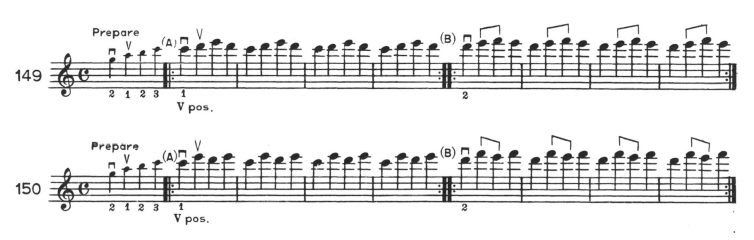

Extending the Fourth Finger

Selected Studies in the Fifth Position

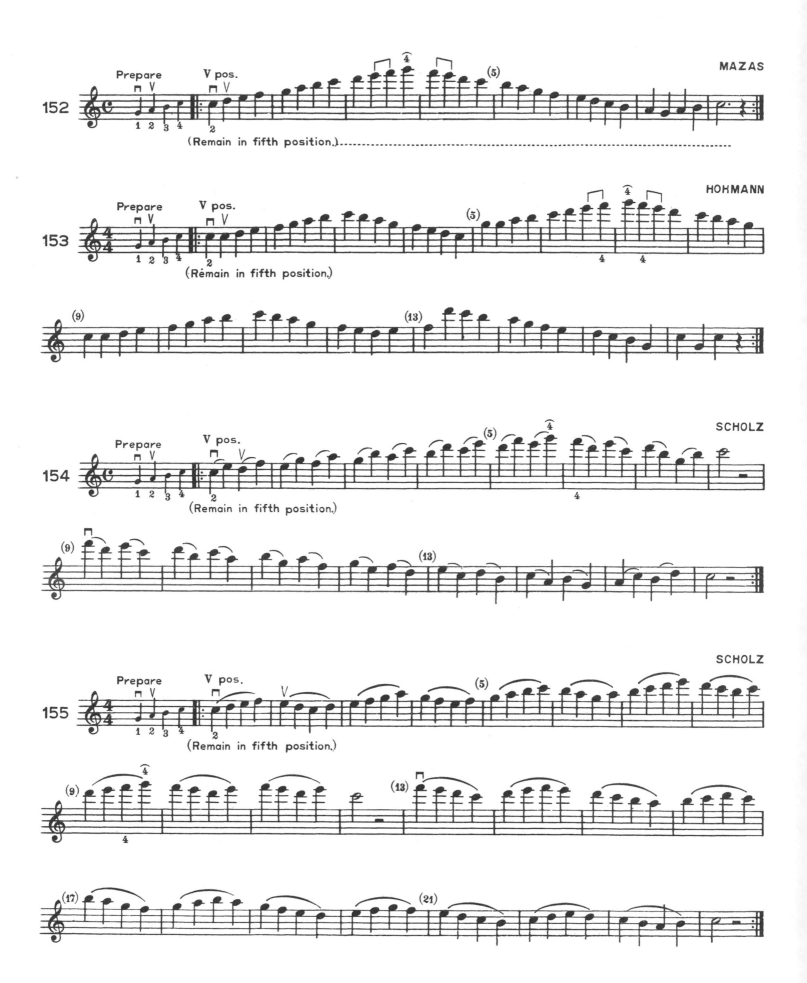

Fifth Position Etude in C Major

SITT

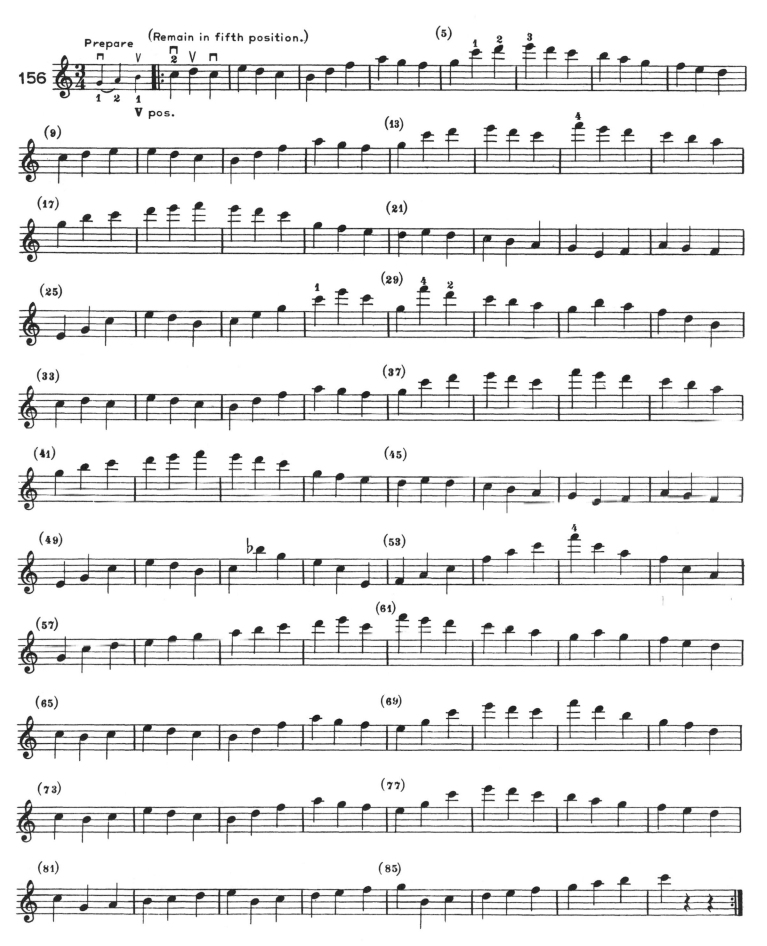

Key of F Major

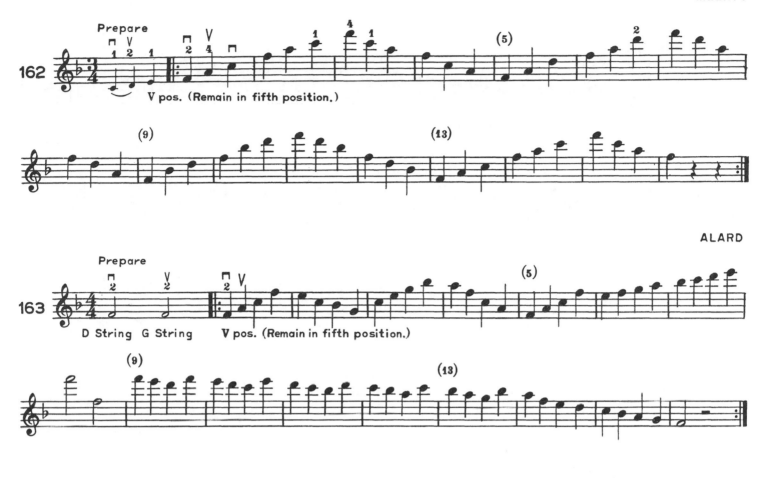

ALARD

Fifth Position Etude in F Major

TOURS

Key of B♭ Major

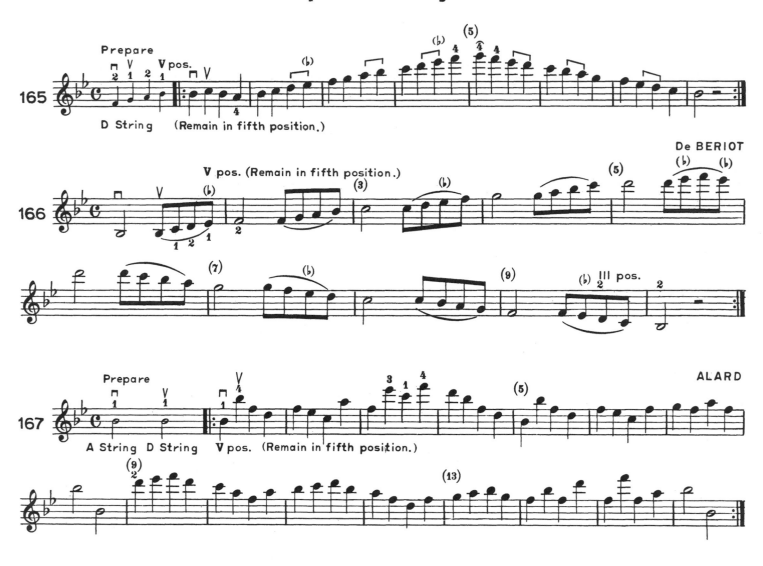

Fifth Position Etude in B♭ Major

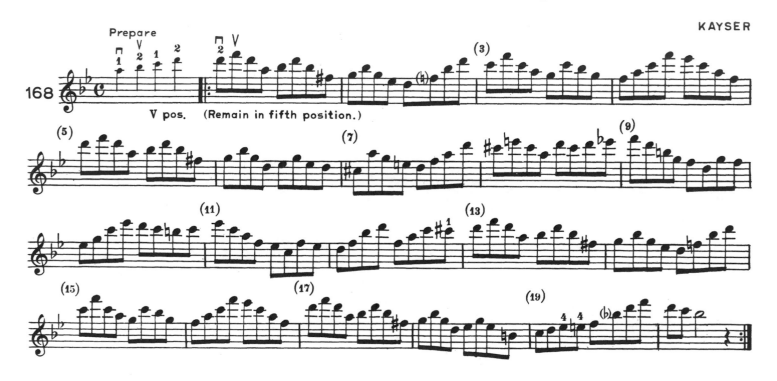

Key of E♭ Major

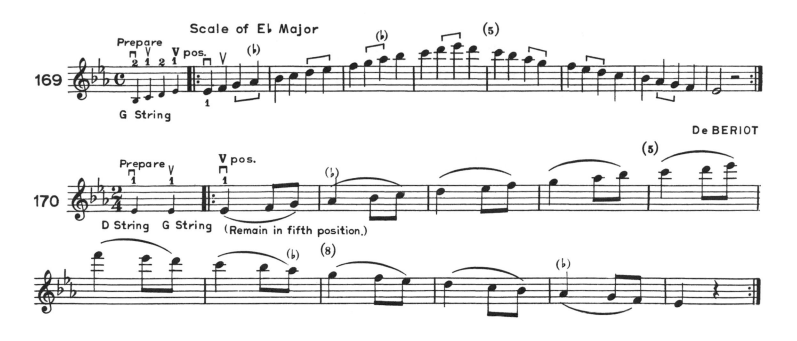

Fifth Position Etude in E♭ Major

Key of G Major

Fifth Position Etude in G Major

KAYSER

Key of D Major

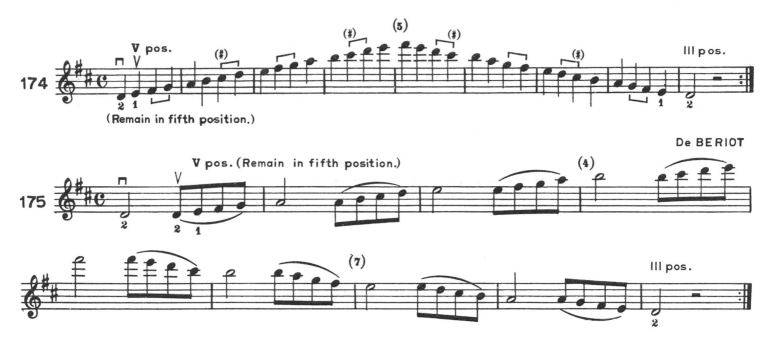

De BERIOT

Fifth Position Etude in D Major

KAYSER

Key of A Major

Fifth Position Etude in A Major

RIES

Shifting from First to Third to Fifth Position

The student should remember to shift forward on the finger that was last down, and likewise, to shift backward on the finger that was last down.

The student also should remember that the small note in the following exercises merely indicates the movement of the finger in shifting, and as the ability to shift from one note to another is perfected, the small note eventually should not be heard.

Shifting from Third to Fifth Position

E String

D String

43

Sevcik Exercises for Shifting the Position

First to Third and Third to Fifth Positions

Dancla Studies in the First, Third and Fifth Positions

Shifting Etude

De BERIOT

Shifting Etude

MAZAS

47

Drink to Me Only With Thine Eyes

Old English Ballad

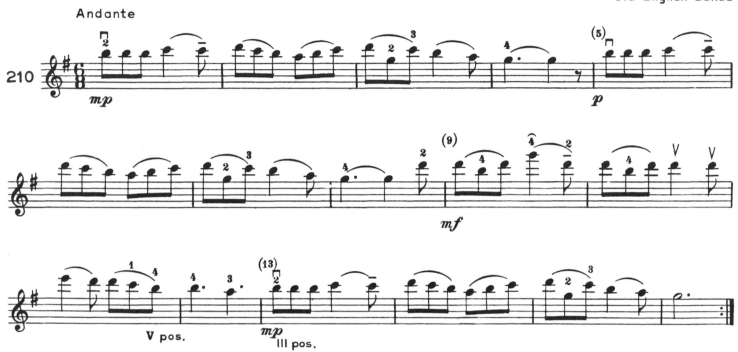

Swanee River

STEPHEN C. FOSTER

On Wings of Song

MENDELSSOHN

Evening Star
from Tannhäuser

WAGNER

Chorales in the First, Third and Fifth Positions
O God, As Divers Aches of Heart

BACH

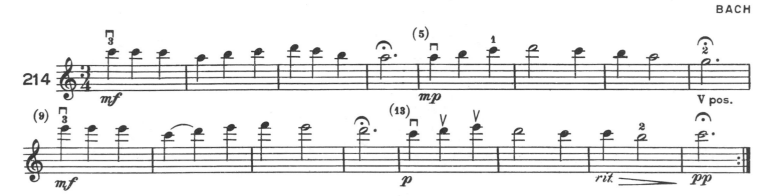

Praise Ye the Lord of Hosts
from "The Christmas Oratorio"

SAINT-SAENS

Thy Name We Hail
from "The Redemption"

GOUNOD

Lord and Master

BACH

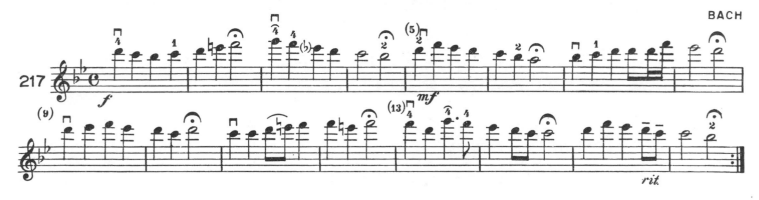

Fantasie-Caprice
Concert Etude in the First, Third and Fifth Positions

De BERIOT